The Infinite Banking System: A Revolutionary Approach to Building Wealth

Daniel Melehi

INTRODUCTION

What is Infinite Banking System?

What is Infinite Banking System?

The Infinite Banking System is a revolutionary approach to building wealth that enables individuals to take control of their finances and become their own bankers. It is a concept that has been around for over a century but has gained popularity in recent years as people look for alternative ways to manage their money.

At its core, the Infinite Banking System is about using a specially designed whole life insurance policy as a vehicle for savings and investment. Whole life insurance is a type of insurance policy that provides both a death benefit and a cash value component that grows over time. This cash value can be borrowed against, used to pay premiums, or withdrawn tax-free.

With the Infinite Banking System, individuals take out a whole life insurance policy and use it to fund their personal banking system. They make regular premium payments, which go towards building the cash value of the policy. They then borrow against this cash value to finance their purchases, investments, and other financial needs.

The benefits of the Infinite Banking System are numerous. First and foremost, it allows individuals to take control of their finances and become their own bankers. They can borrow against their own savings, rather than relying on traditional banks or other financial institutions. This provides them with a greater degree of flexibility and control over their money.

Additionally, the Infinite Banking System is a tax-efficient way to save and invest. The cash value of the whole life insurance policy grows tax-deferred and can be withdrawn tax-free. This means that individuals can use their savings to fund their investments without worrying about taxes eating into their returns.

Finally, the Infinite Banking System provides individuals with a way to build generational wealth. The cash value of the whole life insurance policy can be passed down to future generations tax-free, providing a legacy of financial security and stability.

In conclusion, the Infinite Banking System is a powerful tool for building wealth and taking control of your finances. It provides individuals with a way to become their own bankers, use tax-efficient savings and investments, and build generational wealth. If you are looking for a new way to manage your money and build a secure financial future, the Infinite Banking System may be the solution you have been searching for.

History of Infinite Banking System

The history of the Infinite Banking System dates back to the early 20th century when Nelson Nash, the founder of the concept, realized that the traditional banking system was not serving the best interests of people. Nash, a financial planner and life insurance agent, believed that everyone should have access to a banking system that prioritizes their financial well-being.

Nash's idea of the Infinite Banking System was based on the concept of whole life insurance, which he believed was the best way to build wealth and protect assets. The system involves using whole life insurance policies as a means of creating a personal banking system that allows individuals to borrow against their policies for any purpose they choose.

The Infinite Banking System is based on the idea that individuals can become their own bankers by creating a personal banking system that is separate from the traditional banking system. The system works by using whole life insurance policies as a means of creating a cash reserve that can be accessed for any purpose.

The history of the Infinite Banking System is not without controversy, as some critics argue that it is a form of high-cost life insurance that may not be suitable for everyone. However, advocates of the system argue that it is a revolutionary approach to building wealth that puts individuals in control of their financial future.

Despite the controversy, the Infinite Banking System has gained popularity over the years, with many individuals and businesses adopting the system as a means of building wealth and protecting their assets. The system has also evolved over time, with various strategies and techniques being developed to maximize the benefits of the system.

In conclusion, the history of the Infinite Banking System is a fascinating one that highlights the need for a banking system that prioritizes the financial well-being of individuals. While there may be controversy surrounding the system, it remains a popular approach to building wealth and protecting assets, and its popularity is likely to continue to grow in the years to come.

Benefits of Infinite Banking System

The Infinite Banking System is a revolutionary approach to building wealth that has been gaining popularity in recent years. It is a financial strategy that allows individuals to take control of their finances and create a secure financial future for themselves and their families. The benefits of the Infinite Banking System are numerous and can be enjoyed by anyone who is willing to take the time to learn about it.

One of the key benefits of the Infinite Banking System is its ability to provide individuals with a high degree of financial security. By setting up their own private banking system, individuals are able to protect their assets from market fluctuations and other external factors that could potentially threaten their financial stability. This is achieved by creating a cash reserve that can be used to fund future investments or to cover unexpected expenses.

Another benefit of the Infinite Banking System is its flexibility. Unlike traditional banking systems, which are often rigid and inflexible, the Infinite Banking System allows individuals to customize their financial strategies to meet their unique needs and goals. This means that individuals can tailor their investments to their specific financial situation, which can help them achieve their financial goals more quickly and efficiently.

The Infinite Banking System also offers individuals a way to create a passive income stream. By investing in dividend-paying whole life insurance policies, individuals can receive regular payments that can help supplement their income and provide a source of financial stability. This can be particularly beneficial for individuals who are retired or who are looking to reduce their reliance on a traditional job for income.

Finally, the Infinite Banking System provides individuals with a way to pass on their wealth to future generations. By creating a cash reserve and investing in whole life insurance policies, individuals can build a legacy that will provide for their loved ones for years to come. This can be a powerful way to ensure that one's wealth is preserved and protected for future generations.

Overall, the Infinite Banking System is a powerful financial strategy that offers numerous benefits to individuals of all ages and financial backgrounds. Whether you are looking to build wealth, create a passive income stream, or protect your assets, the Infinite Banking System can help you achieve your financial goals and secure your financial future.

UNDERSTANDING THE INFINITE BANKING SYSTEM

The Concept of Infinite Banking System

The concept of Infinite Banking System is a revolutionary approach to building wealth that has gained popularity in recent years. This system, also known as the Bank On Yourself or Becoming Your Own Banker, allows you to take control of your finances and create a stable and secure financial future.

The Infinite Banking System is based on the idea of using a whole life insurance policy as a vehicle for accumulating wealth. With this system, you can use your life insurance policy as collateral to borrow money from the insurance company at a low-interest rate. This money can then be used to invest in other opportunities or pay off debts.

The beauty of the Infinite Banking System is that you are essentially borrowing from yourself, and the interest payments go back into your policy. This means that you are not only building wealth but also creating a source of passive income. Additionally, the cash value of your policy grows tax-free, and the death benefit is paid out tax-free to your beneficiaries.

One of the main advantages of the Infinite Banking System is its flexibility. You can use the borrowed funds for any purpose, whether it is for a down payment on a house, starting a business, or paying for your child's education. Moreover, you are not subject to the same restrictions and regulations that come with traditional bank loans.

Another benefit of the Infinite Banking System is its predictability. Unlike other investment vehicles, such as stocks or real estate, the cash value of your life insurance policy is not subject to market fluctuations. This means that you can expect a steady and predictable return on your investment over time.

While the Infinite Banking System may not be for everyone, it is a powerful tool for those who are looking for a secure and stable way to build wealth. By taking control of your finances and becoming your own banker, you can create a financial future that is both prosperous and secure.

How Infinite Banking System Works

The Infinite Banking System (IBS) is a revolutionary approach to building wealth that has been gaining popularity in recent years. It is a strategy that involves using a specially designed whole life insurance policy as a financial tool for creating and accessing wealth. The IBS is based on the concept of creating your own personal banking system that allows you to borrow money from yourself, instead of relying on banks or other financial institutions. Here is how the IBS works:

Step 1: Purchase a whole life insurance policy

To implement the IBS, you need to purchase a whole life insurance policy. This policy is designed to provide you with both life insurance coverage and a cash value component that grows over time. The cash value component is what you will use to finance your IBS.

Step 2: Build up cash value

As you pay your premiums, a portion of your payments goes towards the cash value component of your policy. The cash value grows tax-free over time and earns a guaranteed rate of return, which is typically around 4%. This cash value can be accessed through policy loans or withdrawals.

Step 3: Use policy loans to finance your IBS

Once you have built up enough cash value in your policy, you can start using policy loans to finance your IBS. Policy loans are a unique feature of whole life insurance policies that allow you to borrow money against your cash value without having to go through a credit check or pay any interest to a bank. You can use these loans to finance anything you want, such as investments, real estate, or business ventures.

Step 4: Repay the policy loans

When you borrow money from your policy, you are essentially borrowing from yourself. You can repay the loans at any time or let them accumulate if you choose. The interest you pay on policy loans goes back into your policy and helps to grow your cash value, which means you are essentially paying interest to yourself.

Step 5: Continue to build wealth

As you continue to use your IBS, your cash value will continue to grow, and you will have more and more money available to finance your investments and other ventures. Over time, you can use your IBS to build a substantial amount of wealth and achieve financial freedom.

In summary, the IBS is a powerful strategy that allows you to take control of your finances and build wealth on your terms. By using a whole life insurance policy as your personal banking system, you can access your own money, avoid paying interest to banks, and continue to build wealth over time. If you are interested in learning more about the IBS and how it can benefit you, speak with a qualified financial advisor or insurance professional today.

The Role of Insurance in Infinite Banking System

The concept of Infinite Banking System (IBS) is all about creating financial independence by taking control of your money. One of the critical components of this system is insurance, which plays a vital role in ensuring that you have a secure foundation to build upon. In this subchapter, we will explore the role of insurance in the Infinite Banking System and how it can help you achieve financial freedom.

The IBS revolves around the principle of becoming your banker. This means that you leverage your cash value life insurance policy to access funds for loans, investments, or any other financial needs. Insurance is the backbone of the IBS as it provides the necessary funds for borrowing and investing, while also protecting your financial position in case of any unforeseen events.

The type of life insurance policy used in the IBS is known as whole life insurance. Unlike term insurance, which only covers you for a specific period, whole life insurance provides coverage for your entire lifetime. It also has a cash value component, which grows over time and can be used to access funds for loans or investment opportunities.

The cash value in the insurance policy acts as a savings account, which earns interest and grows tax-free. The policyholder can borrow against this cash value at any time, without having to go through a credit check or approval process. This makes it an ideal source of funds for investments or emergencies, as the funds are readily available.

In addition to providing a source of funds, insurance also protects the policyholder's financial position. In the event of death, the death benefit paid out to the beneficiary ensures that their loved ones are financially secure. This protection can also be extended to cover disability, critical illness, or long-term care, depending on the policy purchased.

In conclusion, insurance plays a critical role in the Infinite Banking System. It provides the necessary funds for borrowing and investing while also protecting the policyholder's financial position. Whole life insurance is the preferred type of policy used in the IBS, as it provides lifetime coverage and a cash value component that can be used to access funds. By leveraging insurance in the IBS, individuals can achieve financial independence and take control of their money.

SETTING UP YOUR INFINITE BANKING SYSTEM

Choosing the Right Insurance Policy

Choosing the right insurance policy is a crucial step in the infinite banking system. The right policy can provide you with the necessary security and financial stability to build wealth over time. However, selecting the wrong policy can lead to financial loss and missed opportunities for growth.

The first step in choosing the right policy is to understand the different types of insurance policies available. There are two main types of insurance policies: term and permanent. Term policies provide coverage for a specific period, usually ranging from one to thirty years. Permanent policies, on the other hand, provide coverage for the duration of the policyholder's life.

When selecting a policy, it's essential to consider your financial goals and needs. If you're looking for a policy that provides long-term financial security, a permanent policy may be the best option. However, if you're looking for short-term protection, a term policy may be sufficient.

Another factor to consider when choosing a policy is the premium. This is the amount you'll pay for coverage each month or year. Generally, permanent policies have higher premiums than term policies. However, permanent policies also provide more comprehensive coverage and offer the potential for cash value accumulation.

It's also important to consider the insurance company's financial stability and reputation before choosing a policy. You want to ensure that the company you select has a solid financial standing and a good reputation for customer service.

Finally, it's essential to review the policy carefully before signing. Pay close attention to the terms and conditions, including the coverage limits, exclusions, and any fees associated with the policy.

In conclusion, choosing the right insurance policy is a critical step in the infinite banking system. By considering your financial goals and needs, the premium, the insurance company's stability, and carefully reviewing the policy, you can select a policy that provides the necessary coverage and financial security to build wealth over time.

Funding Your Policy

Funding Your Policy

One of the most vital aspects of implementing the infinite banking system (IBS) is funding your policy. This process is crucial as it determines how much money you can borrow from your policy in the future. However, many people are unsure of how to fund their policies, which is understandable as there are many options available.

Some of the most popular ways to fund an IBS policy include:

1. Lump Sum Payments

Many people choose to fund their policies with a lump sum payment. This involves depositing a large amount of money into your policy at once. This option is ideal for those with extra cash or a windfall.

2. Regular Premiums

Regular premium payments are another popular way to fund IBS policies. This involves making monthly, quarterly, or annual payments to your policy. This option is ideal for those who have a steady income.

3. Paid-Up Additions

Paid-up additions involve purchasing additional insurance coverage within your policy. This option is ideal for those who want to increase the cash value of their policy.

4. Loans

Loans are another option for funding your policy. This involves borrowing money from your policy and paying it back with interest. This option is ideal for those who want to access their policy's cash value without surrendering it.

When funding your policy, it's important to consider your financial goals and needs. It's also important to work with a qualified IBS professional who can help you determine the best funding strategy for your specific situation.

In conclusion, funding your policy is a crucial step in implementing the infinite banking system. By choosing the right funding option for your needs, you can ensure that you have access to the cash value of your policy when you need it most.

Managing Your Policy

Managing Your Policy

Once you have set up your Infinite Banking policy, it is crucial to manage it effectively to maximize its benefits. Managing your policy involves understanding how it works, paying premiums on time, and making informed decisions about loans and withdrawals.

Understanding Your Policy

To manage your policy well, you must first understand how it works. Your policy is a whole life insurance policy that also serves as a savings vehicle. The premiums you pay go towards both the insurance coverage and building cash value. The cash value grows tax-free and can be accessed through loans or withdrawals.

Paying Premiums on Time

To keep your policy in force and maintain its benefits, it is essential to pay your premiums on time. Late payments can result in policy lapses, which means you lose your insurance coverage and access to your cash value. If you miss a payment, it is best to contact your insurance company as soon as possible to make arrangements to bring your policy back into good standing.

Making Informed Decisions About Loans and Withdrawals

One of the most significant benefits of an Infinite Banking policy is the ability to access your cash value through loans or withdrawals. However, it is essential to make informed decisions about these options because they can affect your policy's performance and ultimate benefits.

Loans

When you take out a policy loan, you are borrowing from the cash value of your policy. The loan must be repaid with interest, but the interest goes back into your policy, not to a bank or other lender. This means that you are effectively borrowing from yourself and paying yourself back with interest.

It is important to remember that policy loans can reduce your policy's death benefit and cash value growth. If you do not repay the loan, the outstanding balance and interest will be deducted from your policy's death benefit when you pass away.

Withdrawals

Withdrawing cash value from your policy is another option, but it can also affect your policy's performance. Withdrawals reduce the cash value and death benefit of your policy, and any amount withdrawn above the premiums paid is subject to taxes.

It is essential to consider the impact of withdrawals on your policy's performance and your long-term financial goals before making any withdrawals.

In conclusion, managing your Infinite Banking policy involves understanding how it works, paying premiums on time, and making informed decisions about loans and withdrawals. By managing your policy effectively, you can maximize its benefits and achieve your financial goals.

MAXIMIZING THE POTENTIAL OF YOUR INFINITE BANKING SYSTEM

Investing with Your Infinite Banking System

Investing with Your Infinite Banking System

One of the key benefits of implementing the Infinite Banking System is the ability to use it as a powerful investment tool. By leveraging the cash value of your whole life insurance policy, you can invest in a variety of assets and opportunities, while still maintaining control over your money and protecting your family's financial security.

There are several ways to invest with your Infinite Banking System, including:

Real estate investing: With your policy's cash value as collateral, you can secure loans to purchase rental properties or invest in real estate syndications. This allows you to earn passive income and build long-term wealth, without the risks of traditional financing.

Business financing: If you own a business or are looking to start one, your Infinite Banking System can provide the capital you need to get off the ground or expand. You can use your policy's cash value to secure loans or invest in your business, while still enjoying the benefits of tax-free growth and asset protection.

Stocks, bonds, and mutual funds: While the Infinite Banking System is not designed to be a traditional investment vehicle, you can use it to invest in the stock market or other securities. By borrowing against your policy's cash value, you can take advantage of market opportunities without sacrificing your long-term financial goals.

Alternative investments: From private equity to cryptocurrency, there are many alternative investment options that can be accessed with your Infinite Banking System. By using your policy's cash value as collateral, you can invest in these opportunities while still maintaining control over your money and minimizing risk.

Whatever investment strategy you choose, it's important to remember that the Infinite Banking System is a long-term wealth-building tool. By leveraging the power of compound interest and tax-free growth, you can create a financial legacy that will benefit your family for generations to come.

To get the most out of your Infinite Banking System, it's important to work with a qualified financial professional who understands the unique benefits and strategies of this approach. With the right guidance and support, you can achieve your financial goals and build a life of abundance and security.

Using Your Infinite Banking System for Business

Using Your Infinite Banking System for Business

Business owners often face a dilemma when it comes to managing their finances. They need to keep their finances organized, make sure they have enough cash flow to keep their business running, and ensure they're saving enough for their future. The Infinite Banking System offers a revolutionary approach to managing your finances, including for business owners.

Here are some ways you can use your Infinite Banking System for your business:

1. Financing Your Business

One of the most significant benefits of the Infinite Banking System is that it can help you finance your business. You can borrow money from your policy to fund your business expenses, such as purchasing equipment, hiring employees, or expanding your business. Unlike traditional loans, you won't have to go through credit checks or provide collateral, and the interest rates are typically lower than commercial loans.

2. Managing Your Cash Flow

Cash flow is critical for any business, and the Infinite Banking System can help you manage it effectively. You can use your policy's cash value to cover your business expenses, such as paying bills or payroll, during slow periods. You can also use it to take advantage of investment opportunities or to reinvest in your business.

3. Tax Benefits

The Infinite Banking System offers tax benefits that can help business owners save money in taxes. The policy's cash value grows tax-free, and you can take tax-free loans from it. You can also use it to accumulate wealth that you can use later in life or pass on to your heirs.

4. Retirement Planning

As a business owner, it's crucial to plan for your retirement. The Infinite Banking System can help you do that by providing a source of retirement income. You can use the policy's cash value to supplement your retirement income or to pay for expenses during retirement.

In conclusion, the Infinite Banking System is a powerful tool for managing your finances as a business owner. It offers numerous benefits, including financing your business, managing your cash flow, tax benefits, and retirement planning. By incorporating it into your financial plan, you can achieve financial freedom and build wealth for yourself and your business.

Creating Generational Wealth with Infinite Banking System

Creating Generational Wealth with Infinite Banking System

Infinite Banking System is a revolutionary approach to building wealth that has gained popularity in recent years. It is a financial strategy that allows individuals to become their own bankers and create generational wealth. This system is based on the concept of using whole life insurance policies as a financial tool to build wealth and create a legacy for future generations.

The Infinite Banking System is a unique approach to wealth-building that provides a wide range of benefits to individuals and families. One of the major advantages of this system is the ability to create generational wealth. By using whole life insurance policies as a financial tool, individuals can accumulate significant wealth over time that can be passed down to their heirs.

The key to creating generational wealth with the Infinite Banking System is to start early and be consistent. The system is designed to be a long-term strategy that requires patience and discipline. By making regular contributions to your policy, you can accumulate significant wealth over time that can be used to provide financial security for your family for generations to come.

In addition to providing financial security for your family, the Infinite Banking System also offers tax benefits. The cash value of whole life insurance policies grows tax-free, which means that you can accumulate wealth without paying taxes on the growth. This can be a significant advantage over other investment strategies that require you to pay taxes on your investment earnings.

Another benefit of the Infinite Banking System is the ability to borrow against the cash value of your policy. This allows you to access funds when you need them without having to go through a traditional lender. This can be a significant advantage for individuals who need to access funds quickly for emergencies or unexpected expenses.

In conclusion, the Infinite Banking System is a powerful financial strategy that can help individuals and families create generational wealth. By using whole life insurance policies as a financial tool, individuals can accumulate significant wealth over time that can be passed down to future generations. If you are looking for a long-term wealth-building strategy that provides tax benefits and flexibility, the Infinite Banking System may be the right choice for you.

COMMON MISCONCEPTIONS ABOUT INFINITE BANKING SYSTEM

Debunking Myths about Infinite Banking System

Debunking Myths about Infinite Banking System

Infinite Banking System is a revolutionary approach to building wealth that has been gaining traction in recent years. Despite its increasing popularity, there are still some misconceptions about this concept that need to be debunked. In this subchapter, we will explore some of the most common myths about the Infinite Banking System and explain why they are not true.

Myth #1: Infinite Banking is a scam

One of the most prevalent myths about the Infinite Banking System is that it is a scam. This myth is likely perpetuated by people who do not understand how the system works or who have had a negative experience with a dishonest or unscrupulous financial advisor. However, the truth is that Infinite Banking is a legitimate financial strategy that has been used successfully by many people.

Myth #2: Infinite Banking is only for the wealthy

Another common myth about the Infinite Banking System is that it is only for the wealthy. While it is true that the system works best for people who have a steady income and a substantial amount of money to invest, it is not exclusive to the wealthy. In fact, anyone can use the Infinite Banking System to build wealth, regardless of their income level.

Myth #3: Infinite Banking is too complicated

Some people believe that the Infinite Banking System is too complicated and difficult to understand. However, this is not true. While there are some technical aspects to the system, it is not overly complex. In fact, many people find that the system is easier to understand than traditional financial strategies like investing in the stock market.

Myth #4: Infinite Banking is a get-rich-quick scheme

Another myth about the Infinite Banking System is that it is a get-rich-quick scheme. However, this is not true. The system is designed to help people build wealth over time through careful planning and disciplined saving. It is not a way to make a quick buck or get rich overnight.

In conclusion, the Infinite Banking System is a legitimate and effective way to build wealth. Despite some of the myths that have been perpetuated about the system, it is accessible to anyone and can be used to achieve financial freedom and security. By understanding these myths and debunking them, we can help more people take advantage of this revolutionary approach to building wealth.

Addressing Concerns about Infinite Banking System

Addressing Concerns about Infinite Banking System

The Infinite Banking System has been gaining popularity in recent years as a revolutionary approach to building wealth. However, there are concerns that people have raised about this system. In this chapter, we will address some of these concerns and provide clarity on the Infinite Banking System.

One of the main concerns people have is that the Infinite Banking System is a scam. This is not true. The Infinite Banking System is a legitimate financial strategy that has been used for over a century. It is based on the concept of whole life insurance, which has been around for even longer.

Another concern is that the Infinite Banking System is only for the wealthy. While it is true that people with higher incomes can benefit more from this system, anyone can use it. In fact, the Infinite Banking System is an excellent tool for anyone who wants to take control of their finances and build wealth.

Some people are also concerned that the Infinite Banking System is too complex. While there is a learning curve, the system is not as complicated as it may seem. The basic concept is to use a whole life insurance policy as a savings account and borrowing from it for various expenses.

This allows you to earn interest on your savings while also using it as collateral for loans.

Another concern is that the fees associated with whole life insurance policies are too high. While it is true that whole life insurance policies have higher fees than other types of insurance, the benefits outweigh the costs. Whole life insurance policies provide lifelong coverage and build cash value over time, which can be used for a variety of purposes, including the Infinite Banking System.

Finally, some people are concerned that the Infinite Banking System is too risky. While there is always risk involved with any financial strategy, the Infinite Banking System is relatively low-risk. Since you are borrowing from your own savings, you are not subject to the same risks as borrowing from a bank or other lender.

In conclusion, the Infinite Banking System is a legitimate financial strategy that anyone can use to build wealth. While there are concerns about the system, these can be addressed with proper education and understanding of the system. The Infinite Banking System is an excellent tool for anyone who wants to take control of their finances and build wealth for the future.

Common Mistakes to Avoid with Infinite Banking System

The Infinite Banking System is a unique approach to building wealth that has gained popularity in recent years. It involves using a whole life insurance policy as a financial tool to create a self-sustaining financial system. While this system has proven to be effective for many people, there are some common mistakes that you should avoid to ensure that you get the most out of it.

One of the most common mistakes that people make with the Infinite Banking System is failing to fully understand how it works. This system is not a get-rich-quick scheme, and it requires a long-term commitment. It is important to do your research and understand the mechanics of the system before investing your money in it.

Another mistake that people make is choosing the wrong insurance policy. The whole life insurance policy is the backbone of the Infinite Banking System, and it is crucial to choose the right one. You should look for a policy that has a low premium and a high cash value accumulation rate. This will ensure that you can maximize your returns and build wealth over time.

Another common mistake is failing to make regular premium payments. The Infinite Banking System relies on regular premium payments to build up cash value in the policy. If you miss payments, the system will not work as effectively, and you may end up losing money.

Finally, it is important to avoid taking out loans from your policy too early. While the Infinite Banking System allows you to borrow against your policy, it is important to wait until the policy has built up enough cash value to support the loan. Taking out loans too early can deplete the cash value and weaken the system.

In conclusion, the Infinite Banking System is a powerful tool for building wealth, but it requires careful planning and execution. By avoiding these common mistakes, you can ensure that your system is working effectively and that you are on the path to financial success.

REAL-LIFE EXAMPLES OF INFINITE BANKING SYSTEM

Case Studies of Successful Infinite Banking System Users

The infinite banking system has been gaining a lot of popularity in recent years, and for good reason. This revolutionary approach to building wealth empowers individuals and families to take control of their finances and create a legacy of financial freedom for generations to come.

To illustrate the power of the infinite banking system, let's take a look at some case studies of successful users.

Case Study 1: The Jones Family

The Jones family had been struggling to get ahead financially. They were living paycheck to paycheck and had accumulated significant debt. They decided to implement the infinite banking system and started by taking out a whole life insurance policy on the breadwinner of the family.

Over time, they were able to use the cash value of the policy to pay off their debt, invest in real estate, and fund their children's education. Today, the Jones family has achieved financial freedom and is able to enjoy the fruits of their labor without worrying about money.

Case Study 2: The Smiths

The Smiths were a young couple just starting out in life. They didn't have a lot of money to invest, but they wanted to start building wealth for their future. They decided to implement the infinite banking system and started by taking out a small whole life insurance policy.

Over time, they were able to use the cash value of the policy to invest in stocks, real estate, and other income-producing assets. They also used the system to fund their children's education and pay for their own retirement.

Today, the Smiths have a net worth of over $1 million and are well on their way to achieving financial freedom.

Case Study 3: The Davis Family

The Davis family had always been good with money, but they were looking for a way to take their finances to the next level. They decided to implement the infinite banking system and started by taking out a whole life insurance policy on each family member.

Over time, they were able to use the cash value of the policies to fund their children's education, invest in real estate, and start their own business. Today, the Davis family has achieved financial freedom and is able to enjoy a life of abundance and prosperity.

In conclusion, the infinite banking system has helped countless individuals and families achieve financial freedom and build a legacy of wealth for future generations. These case studies are just a few examples of the power of this revolutionary approach to building wealth. If you're looking for a way to take control of your finances and create a brighter future for yourself and your loved ones, the infinite banking system may be just what you need.

Testimonials from Infinite Banking System Users

Testimonials from Infinite Banking System Users

The Infinite Banking System has been a game-changer for many individuals who were struggling to build wealth and financial security. Here are some testimonials from people who have implemented the Infinite Banking System into their lives:

John, a business owner, says, "I was tired of relying on banks and finance companies to fund my business ventures. I stumbled upon the Infinite Banking System and decided to give it a try. It has been a revelation for me. I now have complete control over my finances and can invest in my business without worrying about high-interest rates or loan approvals."

Mary, a stay-at-home mom, says, "I was always worried about the future and the financial security of my family. The Infinite

Banking System gave me peace of mind as I was able to create a cash reserve that I could use for emergencies or unexpected expenses. It also allowed me to invest in my children's education without relying on student loans or scholarships."

Bob, a retiree, says, "I was looking for a way to generate passive income during my retirement years. The Infinite Banking System allowed me to create a stream of income that I could use to supplement my retirement income. It also gave me the flexibility to access my cash value without penalties or taxes."

These are just a few examples of how the Infinite Banking System has helped individuals achieve financial freedom and security. By creating a cash reserve and investing in yourself, you can take control of your financial future and build wealth on your terms.

The beauty of the Infinite Banking System is that it can be customized to fit your unique financial situation and goals.

Whether you are a business owner, retiree, or stay-at-home parent, the Infinite Banking System can help you achieve your financial goals.

If you are interested in learning more about the Infinite Banking System and how it can benefit you, we encourage you to reach out to a certified Infinite Banking Practitioner. With their expertise and guidance, you can start your journey towards financial freedom and security today.

Benefits of Infinite Banking System for Different Types of People

The Infinite Banking System is an innovative approach to building wealth that has been gaining popularity in recent years. This system is based on the concept of using cash value life insurance policies as a way to create a personal banking system. The benefits of the Infinite Banking System are numerous, and they can be enjoyed by people from all walks of life. In this subchapter, we will explore the benefits of the Infinite Banking System for different types of people.

Entrepreneurs

Entrepreneurs can benefit greatly from the Infinite Banking System. As a business owner, you need access to capital to fund your operations and growth. Traditional financing options can be expensive and risky. With the Infinite Banking System, you can use the cash value of your life insurance policy as collateral for loans. This allows you to access capital quickly and easily, without having to go through the traditional lending process.

Families

Families can also benefit from the Infinite Banking System. One of the key benefits is the ability to create a legacy for your loved ones. By using the cash value of your life insurance policy, you can create a tax-free inheritance for your heirs. This can help to ensure that your family is taken care of financially, even after you are gone.

Retirees

Retirees can use the Infinite Banking System to create a steady stream of income in retirement. By using the cash value of your life insurance policy, you can create a tax-free source of income that is not subject to market fluctuations. This can help to ensure that you have a stable source of income in retirement, without having to worry about market volatility.

Investors

Investors can use the Infinite Banking System to create a tax-efficient investment strategy. By using the cash value of your life insurance policy, you can invest in a wide range of assets, without having to pay taxes on your earnings. This can help to maximize your investment returns, while minimizing your tax liability.

In conclusion, the benefits of the Infinite Banking System are numerous, and they can be enjoyed by people from all walks of life. Whether you are an entrepreneur, a family, a retiree, or an investor, the Infinite Banking System can help you to achieve your financial goals and build wealth.

CONCLUSION

Recap of the Infinite Banking System

The Infinite Banking System is a revolutionary approach to building wealth that has been gaining popularity in recent years. This system is based on the concept of using whole life insurance policies as a means of creating a "banking" system that can be used to finance personal and business ventures.

The basic premise of the Infinite Banking System is that whole life insurance policies provide a unique opportunity to accumulate wealth over time. Unlike term life insurance policies, which only provide coverage for a specified period of time, whole life insurance policies provide coverage for the insured's entire life. This means that as long as the policy remains in force, the insured will have access to the policy's cash value.

The cash value of a whole life insurance policy is essentially a savings account that grows over time. This cash value can be borrowed against at any time, without having to go through a traditional bank. This is where the concept of "infinite banking" comes in. By using the cash value of a whole life insurance policy as a source of financing, individuals and businesses can become their own bank.

The benefits of the Infinite Banking System are numerous. For one, it allows individuals and businesses to have more control over their finances. They no longer have to rely on banks for loans, which can be difficult to obtain and come with high interest rates. Additionally, because the cash value of a whole life insurance policy is not subject to market fluctuations, it provides a certain level of stability that is not available with other types of investments.

Another benefit of the Infinite Banking System is that it can help individuals and businesses build wealth over time. By borrowing against the cash value of a whole life insurance policy, they can invest in other ventures that have the potential to generate a higher return than the interest on the loan. This can result in a significant increase in wealth over time.

In conclusion, the Infinite Banking System is a revolutionary approach to building wealth that is based on the concept of using whole life insurance policies as a means of creating a "banking" system. By using the cash value of these policies as a source of financing, individuals and businesses can become their own bank, which provides numerous benefits, including greater control over their finances, stability, and the potential to build wealth over time.

Benefits of Using the Infinite Banking System

The Infinite Banking System, also known as the Becoming Your Own Banker concept, is a powerful financial strategy that has gained popularity among individuals and business owners. It is a revolutionary approach to building wealth that provides a host of benefits that are unmatched by traditional banking methods.

One of the primary benefits of using the Infinite Banking System is that it allows you to take control of your financial future. By becoming your own banker, you can use your own money to finance major purchases, investments, and even emergencies. This means that you no longer have to rely on traditional banks or lending institutions to access the funds you need.

Another key benefit of the Infinite Banking System is that it provides tax advantages that can help you grow your wealth faster. Because the system is based on a permanent life insurance policy, the cash value that you accumulate is tax-deferred. This means that you can enjoy tax-free growth on your investments, which can help you save a significant amount of money over time.

Perhaps one of the most appealing benefits of the Infinite Banking System is the flexibility that it offers. Unlike traditional banking methods, which often come with strict rules and regulations, the Infinite Banking System allows you to customize your financial plan to meet your specific needs and goals. This means that you can adjust your plan as your financial situation changes, making it a truly versatile and adaptable approach to building wealth.

Another significant benefit of the Infinite Banking System is that it allows you to build a legacy for your family. By using the system to accumulate wealth and pass it down through generations, you can create a lasting financial legacy that can benefit your family for years to come.

Overall, the Infinite Banking System is a powerful financial strategy that offers a host of benefits that are unmatched by traditional banking methods. Whether you are just starting your financial journey or are looking for a new approach to building wealth, the Infinite Banking System can help you achieve your goals and secure your financial future.

Action Plan for Implementing the Infinite Banking System

The Infinite Banking System is a revolutionary approach to building wealth, and it is a concept that has been gaining popularity in recent years. The system is based on the idea of using a whole life insurance policy as a savings vehicle. Through this system, individuals can build wealth, increase their cash flow and gain financial freedom.

If you are interested in implementing the Infinite Banking System, there are a few key steps that you should consider. These steps will help you to create a solid plan for implementing the system and ensure that you are on the path to financial success.

Step 1: Understand the Concept

The first step in implementing the Infinite Banking System is to understand the concept. You need to understand how the system works, how it can benefit you, and what the risks are. You can do this by reading books and articles on the subject, attending seminars or workshops, and talking to experts in the field.

Step 2: Find a Qualified Advisor

Once you have a good understanding of the Infinite Banking System, the next step is to find a qualified advisor. This person should be knowledgeable about the system and should be able to help you create a personalized plan that is tailored to your specific financial goals.

Step 3: Choose the Right Insurance Policy

Choosing the right insurance policy is critical to the success of the Infinite Banking System. You need to choose a policy that has a high cash value, low fees, and a solid dividend history. Your advisor can help you choose the right policy for your needs.

Step 4: Fund Your Policy

Once you have chosen the right policy, the next step is to fund it. You can do this by making regular premium payments, or by making a lump sum payment. Your advisor can help you determine the best funding strategy for your needs.

Step 5: Use Your Policy as a Savings Vehicle

Once your policy is funded, you can use it as a savings vehicle. You can borrow against the cash value of the policy to fund investments or other expenses. By doing this, you can increase your cash flow and build wealth over time.

Implementing the Infinite Banking System takes time and effort, but the rewards can be significant. By following these steps and working with a qualified advisor, you can create a solid plan for building wealth and achieving financial freedom.

APPENDIX

Frequently Asked Questions

Frequently Asked Questions

Here are some of the most commonly asked questions about the Infinite Banking System:

What is Infinite Banking?

Infinite Banking is a financial strategy that allows individuals to become their own bankers. It involves using a specially designed whole life insurance policy as a savings and investment vehicle, which can be used to finance large purchases, pay off debt, and build wealth over time.

How does Infinite Banking work?

Infinite Banking works by using a whole life insurance policy as a savings account. The policy builds cash value over time, which can be borrowed against at any time. When you borrow against your policy, you pay interest to the insurance company instead of a bank. This interest goes back into your policy, which helps it grow even more.

Why use a whole life insurance policy for Infinite Banking?

Whole life insurance policies have a number of unique features that make them ideal for Infinite Banking. They offer guaranteed cash value growth, tax-deferred growth, and death benefits. Plus, the cash value can be borrowed against without triggering taxes or penalties.

Who can benefit from Infinite Banking?

Anyone can benefit from Infinite Banking, regardless of their income level or financial situation. It's a great option for those who want to build wealth, pay off debt, or finance large purchases without relying on banks or other lenders.

Is Infinite Banking a safe and reliable strategy?

Yes, Infinite Banking is a safe and reliable strategy. Whole life insurance policies are backed by highly rated insurance companies, which means that your money is safe and secure. Plus, the cash value growth and death benefits are guaranteed, so you can be confident in your investment.

How do I get started with Infinite Banking?

To get started with Infinite Banking, you'll need to work with a financial professional who is familiar with the strategy. They can help you choose the right whole life insurance policy and set up your Infinite Banking system. With the right guidance, you can start building wealth and achieving your financial goals with this powerful strategy.

Resources for Further Learning

Resources for Further Learning

If you're interested in learning more about the Infinite Banking System, there are many resources available to you. Whether you prefer to read books, watch videos, or attend seminars, there's something for everyone.

Books

One of the best ways to learn about the Infinite Banking System is to read books on the subject. There are several great books out there that go into detail about how the system works and how it can benefit you. Some of the most popular titles include:

- Becoming Your Own Banker by R. Nelson Nash
- The Infinite Banking Concept by L. Carlos Lara and Robert P. Murphy
- The Bank On Yourself Revolution by Pamela Yellen
- Building Your Warehouse of Wealth by R. Nelson Nash

Videos

If you prefer to learn by watching videos, there are plenty of resources available online. You can find videos on YouTube that explain the Infinite Banking System in detail, as well as interviews with experts in the field. Some of the best channels to check out include:

- The Infinite Banking Concept
- Pamela Yellen
- Paradigm Life

Seminars

Attending a seminar is another great way to learn about the Infinite Banking System. You'll have the opportunity to hear from experts in the field, ask questions, and network with other like-minded individuals. Some of the best seminars to attend include:

- Infinite Banking Institute
- Paradigm Life
- Nelson Nash Institute

In addition to these resources, it's also a good idea to connect with others who are interested in the Infinite Banking System. Joining online forums, Facebook groups, and other communities can be a great way to learn from others and get support as you implement the system in your own life.

No matter which resources you choose to use, the most important thing is to keep learning and growing. The Infinite Banking System is a powerful tool for building wealth and achieving financial freedom, and the more you know about it, the better equipped you'll be to make it work for you.

Glossary of Terms.

The Infinite Banking System: A Revolutionary Approach to Building Wealth is a comprehensive guide to the principles and strategies of infinite banking. As you delve into the world of infinite banking, you may come across some terms that are unfamiliar or confusing. To help you navigate this new terrain, we have compiled a glossary of terms that you may encounter as you explore the infinite banking system.

1. Infinite Banking System: A process of utilizing a whole life insurance policy as a financial tool to store and grow wealth over time.

2. Whole Life Insurance: A type of life insurance that provides both a death benefit and a savings component, known as cash value.

3. Dividend: A portion of a company's profits that is paid out to shareholders, often in the form of cash or stock.

4. Cash Value: The savings component of a whole life insurance policy that grows over time and can be used for various financial purposes.

5. Policy Loan: A loan taken against the cash value of a whole life insurance policy.

6. Premium: The amount paid to an insurance company in exchange for coverage.

7. Death Benefit: The amount paid out to beneficiaries upon the death of the insured policyholder.

8. Surrender Value: The amount of cash value that can be obtained upon surrendering a whole life insurance policy.

9. Net Surrender Cost Index: A measure of the cost-effectiveness of a whole life insurance policy, taking into account the surrender value and premiums paid.

10. Paid-up Additions: Additional insurance purchased using the cash value of a whole life insurance policy.

These are just a few of the terms you may encounter as you explore the infinite banking system. By familiarizing yourself with these terms, you can better understand the concepts and strategies behind infinite banking and make informed financial decisions.

Made in the USA
Columbia, SC
07 September 2024

41588004R00039